Usborne
Phonics Readers
Mouse moves house

Phil Roxbee Cox

Illustrated by Stephen Cartwright

Edited by Jenny Tyler

Language consultant: Marlynne Grant
BSc, CertEd, MEdPsych, PhD, AFBPs, CPsychol

There is a little yellow duck to find on every

First published in 2006 by Usborne Publishing Ltd., Usborne House, 83-85 Saffron Hill, London EC1N URT, England. www.usborne.com
Copyright © 2006, 2002 Usborne Publishing Ltd.

Mack the mouse is
moving house.

Mack packs his backpack.

Now Mack packs his plates.

Here is Mack's
friend Jack.

Together, Mack and Jack pack and pack.

Jack packs Mack's
nick-nacks in a
black sack.

It's time to pack
the pictures.

and they stack...

Mack and
Jack pack...

Now Mack is all packed.

"That's that!" says Jack.

Jack helps Mack
put his backpack
on his back.

Mack opens his
door and walks
out onto
the floor.

But Mack stays out.

He chats with the cat.

"Come here, Jack. Meet my friend Fat Cat."

Mack the mouse
is moving house
on Fat Cat's back!